CW01651015

This book belongs to:

Name Louise Campbell

Address ....

....

....

....

Age 9

£3.75

Grandad
Woodruff and his Wife
Grandma
Pip
Daisy

Major
Gorge Heather
and Baby
Mustard
Mr Periwinkle
Conker

the Pondles week
Jumping Sunday
Washing Monday
Toad's Day

Windy Day
Thistle Day
Frisky Day
Splatterday

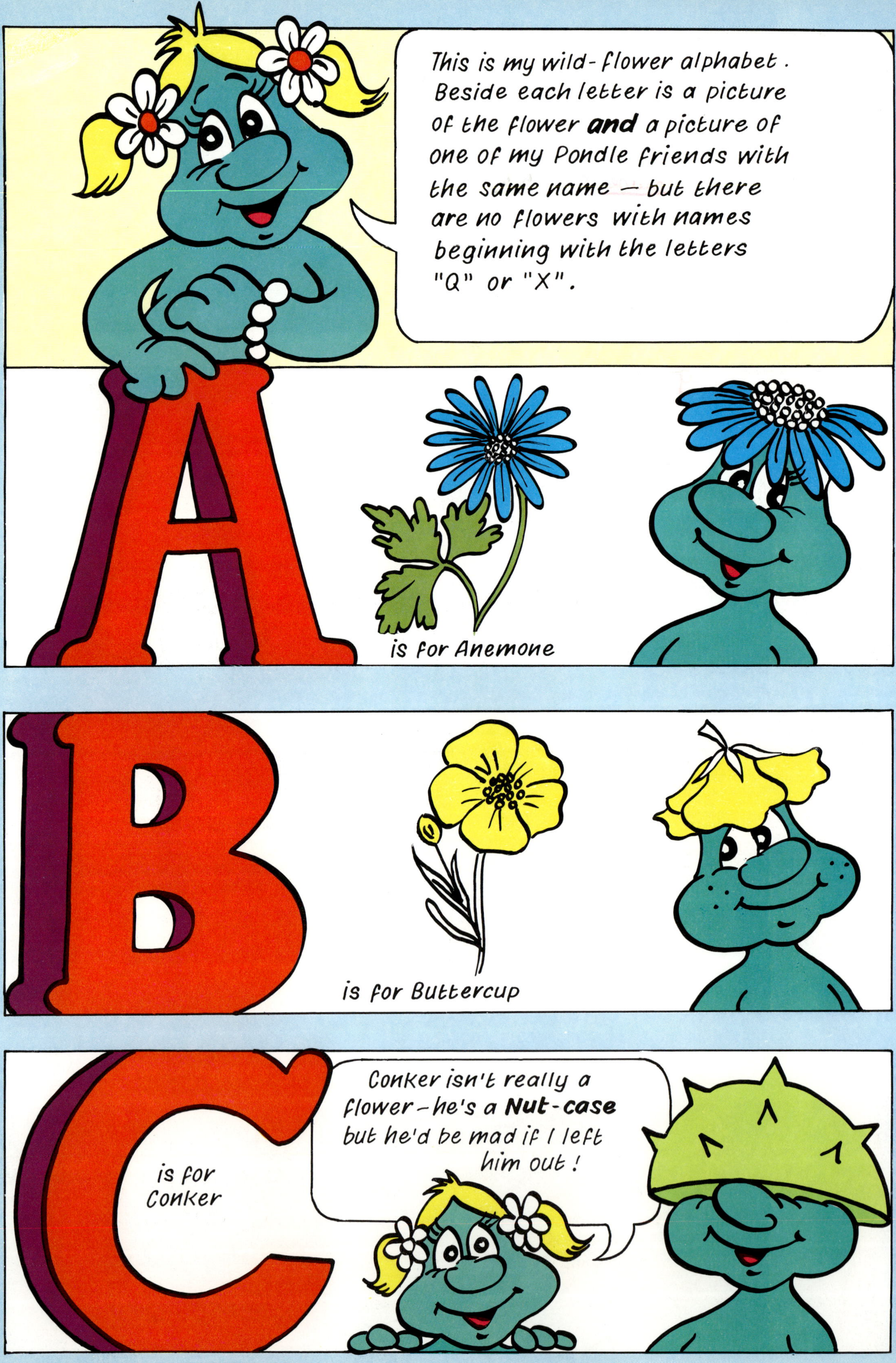
This is my wild-flower alphabet. Beside each letter is a picture of the flower **and** a picture of one of my Pondle friends with the same name — but there are no flowers with names beginning with the letters "Q" or "X".
A
is for Anemone
B
is for Buttercup
C
is for Conker
Conker isn't really a flower — he's a **Nut-case** but he'd be mad if I left him out!

D
That's me!
is for Daisy

E
is for Elderflower

F
is for Flax

G
is for Gorse
H
is for Heather

I is for Ivy

J is for Jersey Thrift

K is for Knot-Grass

L is for Lily-of-the-Valley

M is for Mustard

N is for Narcissus

O is for Orchid

P is for Periwinkle

is for Rattle

is for Samphire

is for Thistle

is for Urtica (Nettle)

V
is for
Violet

W
is for Woodruff

X
Y
is for Yarrow

Z
is for Zig-Zag Clover

Bangers and Mash

the railway song

chorus . . .

Bangers and mash, bangers and mash,
Wave 'bye 'bye to the station master.
Sound the hooter,
Let's go faster, faster,
Off we go on the puffer.

Bangers and mash, bangers and mash,
Over the hills and down the dales,
Through the woods and the forest trails.
Jumping frogs and racing snails.

repeat chorus . . .

Bangers and mash, bangers and mash,
All aboard we're leaving soon.
Clear the tracks and hold on tight,
We'll be back sometime tonight.

a picture for you to colour
1ST CLASS

CATERPILLAR'S YEAR

I find a good strong twig to hang on to. Then I knit myself a nice, cosy cocoon.
After I set my alarm clock for spring, I tie my cocoon to the twig, and climb in.
While I sleep through the winter, my body changes inside my cocoon.
And here I am again the following spring! Yes, it is me . . . but now I am a butterfly. See . . . I can fly - whoopee - no more brown boots for me!

1. One day, Pip and Daisy were walking along when they met Mustard. "Are you going puddle jumping today, Mustard?" asked Pip. "There are lots of puddles."

2. Mustard looked rather sad. "No," said Mustard. "I can't go puddle jumping today. I just can't." The other two Pondles looked very surprised at that. What *did* Mustard mean?

5. . . . not let me have any supper. And I don't want to miss my supper." Pip and Daisy understood. "You are right, Mustard," said Daisy. "We will go and play on our own."

6. Then Pip suddenly smiled and said, "What's for supper today?" "What's today?" said Mustard. "Wednesday," said Daisy. "I know what we have for supper today," said Pip.

3. "Why can't you play today, Musty?" said Daisy, looking very surprised indeed. "Yes," said Pip, "You have got your Wellingtons on. Come and join the fun."

4. Poor Mustard looked even sadder. "It is no use," he said. "I cannot go puddle jumping today. I would really like to, but Mum said that if I got myself muddy she would . . .

7. "What's that?" said the others. *"Cold snail soup!"* said Pip. "Yuk," gasped Mustard. "Yuk, yuk, yuk," went Daisy. Pip gave a great big grin. "What shall we do now?" he said.

8. "Go puddle jumping, of course," said Mustard. So that is what those Pondles did. Mum wasn't pleased when she saw them, but she gave them their supper anyway. Yuk, yuk!

To play this game with a friend, you will need a dice, a pot to shake it in and two counters, one for Pip and one for Daisy. Choose which Pondle each of you wants to be, then, in turn, throw the dice and move your counter the number of spaces shown. If a player's counter lands on a space with words on it, then that player must do what the words say. The one to get home to tea first is the winner.

"Boo!"
Blah! Blah! Blah!
If you land on this space, go this way.
Jackdaw chick says: "Boo!" Go this way.
Have a long, slow talk with turtoise. Miss a turn.
Stop and wait one turn, while Hedgehog crosses.
Stop to take stone out of wellie. Miss a turn.
Toad gives you a lift all the way home!
Stop to eat two dandelion doughnuts. Miss a turn.
Come along you two, time for tea.
HOME

Poor Daisy is in danger of being pinched by one of the nasty Jackdaws. "Which path should I take to take me back to Puddle Town?" says Daisy. "Try and choose the right path first time. I don't want to meet a nasty old Jackdaw!"

Here are eight Pondle things for you to make into four pairs that go together. Here are some clues to help you. Remember what Conker likes eating, where toads like to sit, where furniture belongs and who needs an alarm clock.

THE PURPLE THINGAMABOB

PIP had been very quiet all through breakfast. "Is something wrong, Pip old lad?" asked Grandad.

"I'm bored, Grandad. That's what's wrong," answered Pip. "I'm bored being just another ordinary Pondle. Look at us! We're all the same: two eyes, a nose, a mouth, and a pair of wellies. I wish I could be something different."

"D'you mean you'd like to be a hedgehog or a grasshopper or a tree?" said Daisy.

"No Daisy. Nothing like that. I mean something really *unusual!* What do you think, Grandad?" sighed Pip.

"Well, I'm happy to be a Pondle," began Grandad. "But I'll tell you this, Pip. I should be very careful about wishing to be too different. What if your wish were granted, eh? I mean you might wake up one morning and find you're – you're *The Purple Thingamabob!"*

"The Purple Thingamabob," repeated Pip. "What's that, Grandad?"

"To tell the truth, Pip – I haven't seen it myself," Grandad admitted. "But I've heard that this thing looks like a Pondle. Except it's a sort of purple colour. And it's bad. Oh yes. It's really bad!"

"What do you mean – bad, Grandad?" asked Daisy.

"I mean bad like it'll step on your toes. I mean bad like it'll tickle your tum. Bad because it makes 'orrible faces. Very, very 'orrible. That's what I mean!" explained Grandad. "If I were you Pip, I'd go out and play and forget all about being something different."

Long before Pip and Daisy were up and about, other Pondles were busy picking pondleberries and placing them in a big cart. And very carefully too. Because if you crush the berries, they stain your hands and clothing.

Later, they'd wheel the cart around Puddle Town and every family would get a share of berries to make jam and tarts and pies. But right now, the cart was full and the pickers went home to enjoy a big breakfast.

Pip was walking among the pondelberry bushes, lost in a dream. Thinking about all the things he'd rather be than a Pondle. Without looking where he was going, Pip walked up a plank and fell head over heels into the pondleberry cart. He spluttered and splashed about, crushing the ripe, juicy pondleberries and staining himself a very bright – PURPLE!

"Eeeek!" screamed Daisy in fright. "It's the Purple Whatchermecallit! The Purple Thingamajig! The Purple Whatsit! Whatever it is – EEEK!" And off she ran!

Pip looked at his purple hands and purple tum and was rather pleased with them. Only this morning he wished he could be really different. Now he was!

The first Pondles he met were Heather and Gorse Pondle. Pip greeted them cheerfully. "Hello Heather. Hi Gorse."

Heather and Gorse stared at Pip. They froze in horror – so frightened they couldn't move. Then, together they shouted, "Run for your lives, everyone! It's the Purple Thingamabob!" And off they ran.

Even his pal Mustard acted strangely when he saw Pip. Instead of greeting Pip with a friendly, "Hello Purpleface," Mustard dived into a nearby dustbin and pulled the lid shut.

If his best friend didn't know him, who could Pip turn to for help? Grandad, that's who! "I'll see Grandad at his shed. He'll know what to do," said Pip to himself.

But when Grandad – at the window of his shed – saw Pip coming down the path, he drew back in fear. "Cor! Pondle my soul! It's him! It's The Purple Thingamabob!" he gasped.

"Don't panic, Grandad. It's me, Pip. I fell into a cartful of pondleberries and got stained with pondleberry juice. that's why I'm purple," said Pip.

Grandad opened the shed window and looked at Pip very carefully. "Oh yes. It *is* you, Pip. Oh dear. You certainly got your wish, didn't you! You *are* different!" he said.

"I know, Grandad," said Pip. "But I never wanted to be *this* different. What can I do?"

"Very tricky, getting rid of pondleberry stain, Pip," replied Grandad. "I'll try to think of something. In the meantime, you take this mirror and look at yourself from time to time. Maybe the colour will fade away."

Pip looked at himself in the mirror. What a sight! No wonder he frightened everyone he met. A purple Pondle was a fearsome thing indeed!

He wandered aimlessly down the path to Grimly Woods. Suddenly, something stirred behind a big bush. And then – out leapt the most terrifying creature Pip had ever seen. A creature that was purple from head to toe!

It charged straight at Pip and stamped on his toe! It drew back and charged again. This time, waving a long feather to and fro. The Thing tickled Pip's tum.

Now he remembered Grandad's words at breakfast . . . "IT'S BAD, PIP. I MEAN BAD LIKE IT'LL STEP ON YOUR TOES! BAD LIKE IT'LL TICKLE YOUR TUM AND BAD BECAUSE IT MAKES 'ORRIBLE FACES! IT'S THE PURPLE THINGAMABOB!"

And sure enough, the next thing The Purple Thingamabob did was to screw up its face into the most horrible faces you can imagine. And step by step it was getting closer and closer!

"I wish I could scare that thing the way it's frightening me," thought Pip. Then he had an idea! He held up Grandad's mirror as The Purple Thingy was almost on top of him. "There you are! Take a look at *that!*"

The Purple Thingamabob stopped in his tracks. He stared at his own reflection in the mirror and shrieked, "Mummy! Mummy!" and off he ran.

Pip was glad to be rid of The Purple Thingy. But he still looked like that awful creature. How could he rid himself of this purple colour? He walked on and on but couldn't think of an answer.

In a little while, he arrived at the Puddle Town railway station. He walked out on to the platform and paused under the hose of the big water tank.

Pip looked along the platform. There was his pal, Conker! "Hi, Conk! It's me, Pip!" he called out.

"Cor! It's The Purple Thingy!", cried Conker in alarm. "You go away right now or I'll pull this water chain and pour water all over you!"

"It really *is* me, Conker," said Pip. "Come closer and you'll see." But Conker was as good as his word. He pulled the water tank chain, a flood of water poured down – *and washed all the purple colour off Pip!*

"Crikey!" said Conker. "It really is you!" Then, sorry that he hadn't recognised his good friend Pip, Conker added, "'Course, I was just pretending to be scared, Pip. Anyway, I don't really believe there is such a thing as a Purple Thingamabob!"

But even as he spoke, the two Pondles heard an evil laugh from behind the water tank and a voice hissed, "Oh yes there is!"

Pip and Conker ran all the way home. And the first thing Pip said to Grandad was, "I've changed my mind, Grandad. I *like* being just another ordinary Pondle!"

PONDLE PETS

Do you have a pet? Perhaps you have a Dog, or a Cat, or a Hamster. The Pondles have pets too. You may think they are rather funny ones...

I have a pet Worm called Wilbur, who is exactly one Pondle-meter long, and helps me to measure things correctly!

I found a fat baby Bird who had hurt his toe – so I'm looking after him until he's well enough to fly off. I call him Chirpy – and he likes Dandelion Doughnuts – Just like me!

THE RAIN DANCE....

I T was the loveliest summer anyone in Puddle Town could remember. The sun shone *every* day and it never rained. The Pondles sunbathed, or went for long lazy walks, stopping to have a picnic under the warm sun.

"What wonderful weather!" they said. "Wonderful? WONDERFUL?" muttered the flowers in Heather and Gorse's garden. "Just take a closer look at *us!* There's been no rain for so long, we're dropping all over the place!"

"Oh, dear! The Great Puddle is drying up!" said Mustard Pondle. "Without it, there will be no puddle jumping contests – and no splashing about in wellies!"

Mustard, who measures *everything,* ran off to measure the Puddle. Then he measured it a second day – and a *third.*

There was no doubt about it, the puddle was definitely getting shallower. The flowers at the side of the pond were now becoming incredibly droopy and the water only came up as high as Mr. Newt's knees. "This will not do," said Mr. Newt. "We must have some rain soon."

"CROAK! Someone had better think of a way to fill up this pond with water," grumbled Frog. "I have no where to practise my diving."

"Perhaps I could do a Rain Dance?" said Pip to Mustard. "That might work." But Mustard just stared at the puddle and shook his head.

Mustard didn't listen. "I must tell every one in Puddle Town what is happening," he said as he ran to the Town Hall.

"Er, is something the matter?" asked Major Puddle.

"Y-yes!" he finally managed to gasp. "The G-Great P-Puddle is drying up!"

"You mean . . . " began Barley the Baker.

"Exactly!" interrupted Mustard. "Without the Puddle, we'll have no more puddle jumping!"

"Even more important than that," gasped Major Pondle. "Without The Puddle, we'll have to change our name from *Puddle Town* to – oh, I don't know –perhaps *Muddle Town!"*

"Er, excuse me," said a little voice from the back of the hall. "Perhaps we can do what the American Indians did!"

"Um, yes – exactly!" said Major Pondle, who really didn't have a clue what the American Indians did. "Why don't you explain what they did, Pip. "Just so that the, um, other Pondles here understand."

Pip made his way to the front of the crowd inside the Town Hall. He cleared his throat and spoke up loud and clear so that everyone in the Town Hall could hear. "Well, the American Indians always did a rain dance and it always rained and everything was all right after that."

"Fancy the Pondles dancing around like American Indians," laughed the other Pondles. Mustard thought it was a splendid idea. He remembered reading something about rain dancing in one of his many books.

So at the end of the morning, nothing had been decided. The Major called an end to the meeting and all the Pondles filed out of the Town Hall and went their separate ways. The sun continued to shine on Puddle Town and there was no hint of rain.

At the next meeting, Mustard gave the other Pondles a warning. "The Great Puddle has almost disappeared!" he cried. "Something must be done!"

Woodruff Pondle stood up. "I have been awake all night," he yawned, "thinking about how to make it rain. I think we ought to try-out Pip's idea. But, instead of doing a Rain Dance, we could do a minuette. That might work."

"I suppose it's worth a try," said Major Pondle. So the musicians began to play their fiddles and flutes and the Pondles chose partners. Under the bright sun,

they danced – a funny sort of dance it was, too.

Then they stopped and waited – *nothing!* Not a single drop of rain fell!

"That kind of strange dancing is no good," said Burdock Pondle. "You want to do a Fox Trot. That'll make it rain."

"Very well. Change partners and do the, um, Dog Trot, was it?" said Major Pondle, who was very hard of hearing.

"Fox Trot!" said Burdock. Still nothing happened. The sun still shone.

Bramble Pondle, who leads a band called The Bumpers, shook his head and said: "No – you've got it all wrong. If you want to make it rain, you need a beat – like this!"

Before the other Pondles knew what was happening, band-leader Bramble began waving his baton and his band struck up a tune. They played every kind of music you could possibly think of – jazz, country and western, reggae, rock 'n' roll – the lot!

Puddle Town was really jumping. When everyone was exhausted, they stopped – and listened. *Still no rain!*

Now Grandad Pondle stepped forward. "Right!" he said. "You've all had your say. Now I'll have mine! I say, give Pip a chance. Let's all do a *proper* Rain Dance - just like American Indians!"

"Go ahead, Pip," said Major Pondle. "Do your Rain Dance." "Me? Now?" stammered Pip, who hadn't thought about doing the Rain Dance all by himself – not with everyone else watching him!

Still, there was no way out. How the other Pondles laughed as Pip danced and chanted, as he made his way around the green. All that whooping and shouting and dancing looked very strange indeed.

After five turns around the green, Pip reckoned he'd done enough and stopped to catch his breath.

I'm afraid that was our last chance," sighed Major Pondle, as he looked up at the clear sky. "Thank you for trying, Pip, but . . . "

Major Pondle never finished what he was going to say, because he was interrupted by a *plop! plop!*

It came from The Great Puddle!

Holding their breaths, the Pondles turned. Yes, there *was* a small ripple on the Puddle! Then they heard another PLOP! And another ripple appeared. Suddenly, it was *raining!* Not just raining – it was POURING!

The Pondles jumped up and down, clapped and cheered, patted each other on the back and whooped with delight.

Everyone was so excited they danced around all day in the pouring rain and soon they were all puddle jumping again. Both the frog and Mr. Newt came back to the puddle and swam around in the fresh rain water.

Mustard held his ruler in the puddle and watched as the water level returned to normal. All the Pondles cheered and cheered.

Pip was very popular after that. Bramble and the Bumpers wanted to make a special Rain Dance record and many of the younger Pondles asked Pip to teach them the rain dance steps.

But teaching *everyone* how to do the Rain Dance, wasn't a good idea.

"You see, Pip," smiled Grandad, "if everyone started doing the Rain Dance every time they felt like it, what do you think would happen?"

"They – they could cause a flood!" gasped Pip. "I hadn't thought of that!"

"Right!" grinned Grandad. "Maybe you could teach them how to make a wigwam instead, eh?"

SPRING

During the different seasons of the year you can see different birds and animals when you are out walking. On the next few pages you can write down the birds and animals you see.

BIRDS

ANIMALS

SUMMER

BIRDS

ANIMALS

AUTUMN

WINTER

BIRDS

ANIMALS

Woodland songs

Bats in a tower,
Birds in a nest,
Owl says it's time,
He had a rest.
Woodland folk play all day long in Puddle Town.

Frog's on a log,
Toad's on a stool,
They went for a swim,
And jumped in the pool.
Woodland folk play all day long in Puddle Town.

Fish in the river,
There goes a Bream,
Dragon flies a buzzing,
Is it all a dream?
Woodland folk play all day long in Puddle Town.

A picture to colour

Here are some Pondle riddles for you to try out on your friends.

Why did the Pondle look over the wall?
Because it couldn't see through it.

Can a Pondle jump higher than a tree?
Yes. Because a tree cannot jump.

Why is the letter 'e' lazy?
Because it is always in bed.

When are Grandad's shoes like the sun?
When they shine.

What coat has no buttons?
A coat of paint.

Why did the bus stop?
Because it saw the Zebra Crossing.

When do Pondles have eight legs?
When there are four of them.

Which Pondle wears the biggest hat?
The one with the biggest head.

When does Daisy sound unkind?
When she beats eggs.

What works best on its head?
A broom.

Why is the Pondle postman like a clothes line?
Because he goes from post to post.

Which animals have twelve spotted legs?
Three spotted dogs.

Why does a duck go 'quack'?
It would be silly if it went 'woof'.

Which is the fastest vegetable?
The runner bean.

The naughty Jackdaws have hidden Grandad's best wellies! Before you colour this picture, can you find them for him? The old ones he is wearing, leak when he goes puddle jumping!

POTTING with the PONDLES

Then you put them in a cool dark place, and leave them for several weeks!
And check up on them from time to time, to make sure that the soil doesn't get too dry!
In the spring, you will have pots full of lovely flowers!
But **do** remember to plant the bulbs the right way up. One Autumn Conker planted some upside down by mistake – and in the Spring he found that his **Crocuses** had **Croaked!**
Cor! Did **I** do that?
HELP!

CATERPILLAR SONG

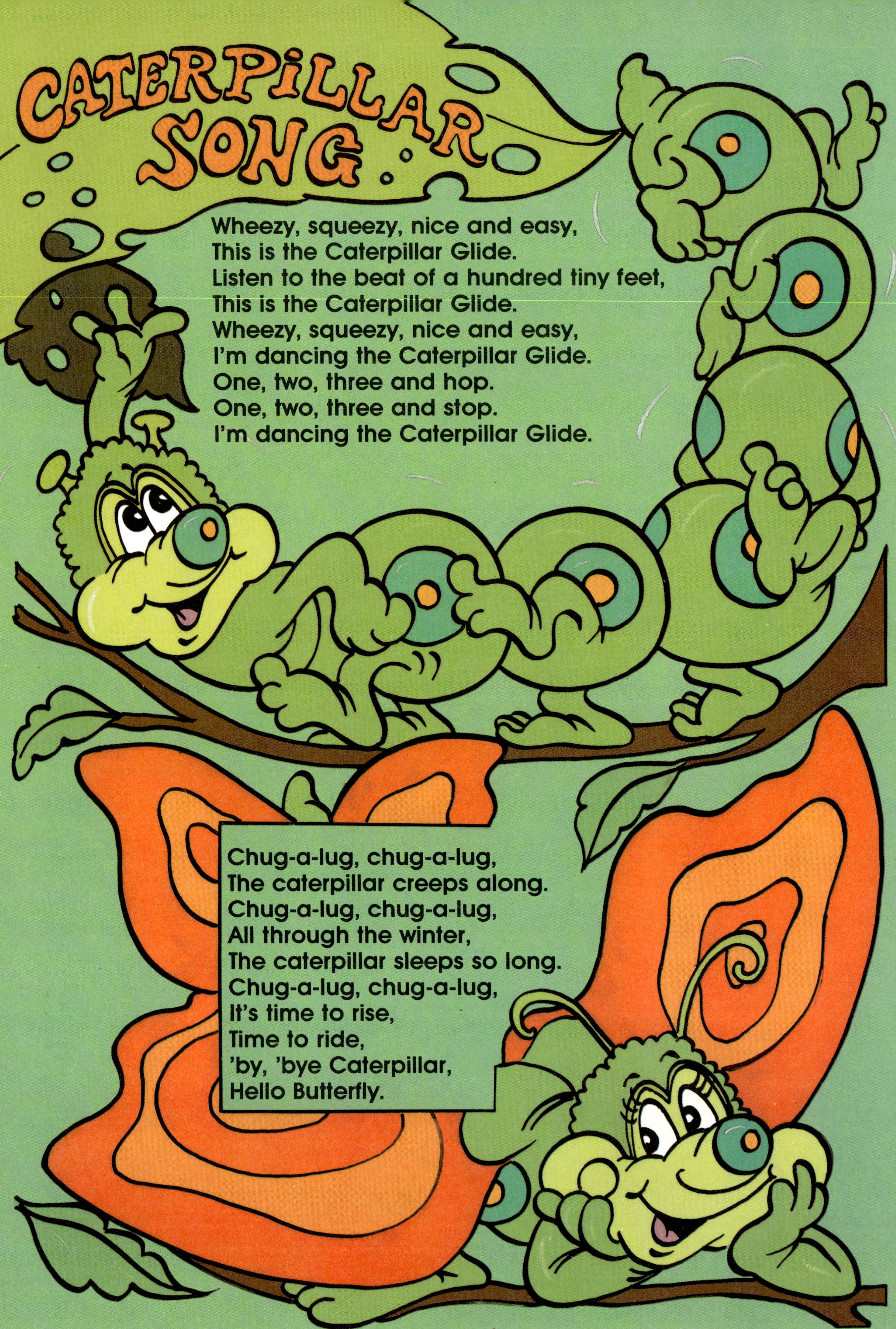

Wheezy, squeezy, nice and easy,
This is the Caterpillar Glide.
Listen to the beat of a hundred tiny feet,
This is the Caterpillar Glide.
Wheezy, squeezy, nice and easy,
I'm dancing the Caterpillar Glide.
One, two, three and hop.
One, two, three and stop.
I'm dancing the Caterpillar Glide.

Chug-a-lug, chug-a-lug,
The caterpillar creeps along.
Chug-a-lug, chug-a-lug,
All through the winter,
The caterpillar sleeps so long.
Chug-a-lug, chug-a-lug,
It's time to rise,
Time to ride,
'by, 'bye Caterpillar,
Hello Butterfly.

Here is a picture to colour of Caterpillar knitting his cocoon for the winter . . .

1. Dig, dig, dig, went Mole. Under the ground he went, and then up he came again. muttering and looking puzzled, he searched.

2. "Tut, tut," he said. "This isn't it!" Dig, dig, dig, went Mole, searching and searching. It is a very hard life being a mole.

5. Up above the ground he poked his head, looking this way and that. "No," he sighed. "It isn't here either. Where can it be?"

6. Just then, along came Pip. "Hello, Mole," said Pip. Suddenly, Mole gave a great big grin. "Hooray! I've found it," he cheered.

3. Bump! Mole dug into a large stone. "Perhaps this is it," he thought. But it wasn't. So off he went again, dig, dig, dig.

4. Mole went digging all over the place. "I just can't remember where it is," he muttered, digging again.

7. Mole looked so pleased, that Pip was sure he had found something exciting. "What have you found? Show me," he said.

8. Mole turned and said, "I have found my front door. Do you know, I have been looking for it all morning.

Pip's Day.

Wakey wakey!
Breakfast-time
Off to school
Jumping lessons with Toad
Knitting lesson with Caterpillar

Lunch-time
Woodcraft with Squirrel
School is out-time for play
Tea-time
Tidy Grandad's shed
Time for bed

The Hedgehog's song

A hedgehog's not a chatty bloke.
For weeks no word I utter.
And when I finally choose to speak,
I only . . . mutter, mutter, mutter.

The ladies they go wild over me,
Their hearts are all a-flutter.
"Oh speak to me of love," they cry.
But I only . . . mutter, mutter, mutter.

I live on fruit and berries and nuts,
And jars of peanut butter.
I never speak when my mouth is full,
I only . . . mutter, mutter, mutter!

Peanut
Butter
Peanut
Butter